The Collector's Workbook

The Collector's Workbook

Projects and ideas for
displaying your treasures

Jayne Keeley

COLLINS & BROWN

To my family and friends

First published in Great Britain in 2000
by Collins & Brown Limited
London House
Great Eastern Wharf
Parkgate Road
London SW11 4NQ

1 3 5 7 9 8 6 4 2

British Library Cataloguing-in-
Publication Data:
A catalogue record for this book
is available from the British Library.

ISBN 1 85585 817 7 (hardback edition)
ISBN 1 85585 847 9 (paperback edition)

Editor **Kate Haxell**
Designer **Ruth Hope**
Photography **Ling Wong**
Illustrations **Jayne Keeley**

Reproduction by Classic Scan Pte Ltd, Singapore
Printed and bound in Hong Kong by Dai Nippon
Printing Co. (HK) Ltd

contents

introduction

We all have sentimental ephemera around us; even the most ardent minimalists have trivia that they can't bring themselves to throw away. Personally, I collect all kinds of things, from sweet papers and stamps to fabrics and trimmings. I can't resist a pretty salt cellar (even if the lid is missing), or a bag of odd buttons. It seems a shame to throw away useful-looking wire or an earring that has lost its mate. I squirrel these things away, waiting for the day I will use them. Now that day has come: in this book there are ideas and projects for making new uses of all kinds of old trivia. You can make unique pieces for the home and personalised gifts for friends and family. Turn an old cheese grater into a candle sconce that sheds the most wonderful light or use safety pins and assorted beads to make sparkling napkin rings. Short lengths of mismatched ribbon can be combined in a decorative heart, or a much-loved sweater with sadly worn elbows can be reincarnated as a cushion.

You don't need to be expert to achieve any of these projects. They are straightforward to do and most do not require specialist materials or tools. Most of us collectors usually admit our obsession with a guilty sigh, but I think it is time to celebrate collecting as an art and, quite literally, make the most of it. So, take pride in your old 'junk' and instead of pushing it back into your cupboards, get it out, use it and enjoy it.

Jayne Keeley

where to collect

There are no shortages of places to collect in. I rummage in junk and antique shops or fairs for curious things, most of which can be bought with the change in your pocket, they cost so little. When purchasing a more expensive piece always barter, or take someone with you who will. My sister, Sam, is a champion haggler and never loses her nerve, often getting prize bargains. Recycling for me is not about penny pinching, it is a way of being more creative with the materials you have. It is deeply satisfying to transform an item that has been found while sifting through a bargain box. It may have been overlooked by many, but with just a little imagination it can be made into something fresh and amazing. Over the years I have built up quite a collection of blue and white china. I started out with a few pieces of 'Yuan' and have also collected 'Willow' and other various patterns: their only thing in common is that they are blue and white. If I break a piece, I use the shards in mosaic work, (see *mosaic place mat*, p106).

Most of my collections have not started out through any conscious decision, they have evolved from one beautiful or interesting object, maybe picked up on a holiday for display at home. It usually isn't long before family and friends see you as a collector and then they will give you pieces to add to your collection. Remember, anything more than two constitutes a collection, so think wisely before you display an item, as you could be starting a colony.

LEFT Antique shops often sell an eclectic range of items, from old rolling pins to lavender sachets. ABOVE Shops selling old enamel-ware are some of my favourites. RIGHT I spend hours in front of displays of blue and white china, looking for pieces to add to my large collection.

storing
collections

If you have collected lots of bits and pieces, it can be hard to keep track of where things are. This is frustrating when you need to lay your hands on a particular item in seconds rather than hours, so it is a good idea to get things into some kind of order. I like to store collections of objects in transparent containers, so that I can identify their whereabouts at a glance. This can also be visually interesting and inspiring. Rows of preserve jars, kitchen containers, sweet jars, bottles and clear plastic boxes are all great for this purpose. Otherwise, I like to put the collections inside boxes decorated with relevant materials. For example, a way of keeping buttons together would to be to decorate the box containing them with buttons glued to the outside, or you could just decorate the lid if you like. Do something similar with postage stamps glued onto a box to keep all your stamps together in. Biscuit tins are often air-tight and are handy for holding various odd and ends. Shoe boxes can be covered with wallpaper or fabric remnants to make decorative homes for swatches and scraps. Use old type-setting trays to store tiny objects; they can be hung on the wall, where they will be both pretty and practical. Look for larger pieces of furniture, such as haberdasher's drawers, which are great for storing fabrics and linen.

RIGHT Assorted jars and boxes provide accessible, and decorative, storage for collections of small items.

displaying collections

Once you have picked up a number of items from the same 'family', consider displaying them while you are waiting for inspiration for a new use for them. Individually, they may look nothing out of the ordinary, but put with other similar, but varying, items, they take on a new lease of life. This collection of glass condiment holders has been put on a windowsill, so light bounces off their reflective surfaces. Some of the containers have long ago lost their lids, but this doesn't matter. I filled them with little sprigs of favourite flowers, turning them into tiny vases. Glass candlesticks, with or without candles, are also shown to advantage in a window. They do not need to be in matching pairs to look good, in fact their varying colours and styles add to the charm of the whole display.

ABOVE A common material – glass – unites this display of otherwise mismatched candlesticks.
RIGHT Items don't have to be perfect to be decorative, as this display of condiment holders shows.

buttons
& beads

My button and bead collections started
with my grandmother's hoarding tins. She had
lived through times when recycling was a way of
life and she kept absolutely everything.
When I was a child I could sometimes persuade
her to empty the tins out onto a large table top
and let me play with the contents.
In among the rusty keys, elastic bands and bits of
string, I would discover crystal or pearl buttons,
little 'gems', broken strings of beads and odd
earrings, all of which were great treasures to me.
In this chapter I have tried to find a use
for all of these pretty things with projects for
matched and mismatched buttons and
beads of all shapes and sizes.

ABOVE Button and rose heart, page 34.

*LEFT Two button
picture frames,
page 28.
ABOVE Beaded
napkin ring,
page 18.
RIGHT Buttoned
cuffs & cushion,
page 24.*

buttoned pin-cushion

A little girl's outgrown denim dress was the starting point for this heart pin-cushion, though you could use a scrap of any favourite garment: it would look lovely in velvet for instance. Decorate the pin-cushion with the recipient's initial or a simple heart shape picked out in mother-of-pearl buttons. Make one for yourself and keep it to hand when you stitch fresh additions for your wardrobe.

YOU WILL NEED

Heart template, page 124

Pencil

Denim fabric measuring
20 x 40cm (8 x 16in)

Pinking shears

Buttons

Striped fabric measuring
7 x 50cm (2³⁄₄ x 20in)

Pins

Needle

Thread

Stuffing

1 Enlarge the template to the required size and draw around it in pencil onto the back of the fabric. Cut out two heart shapes with pinking shears.

3 Draw a pencil line 1cm (¹⁄₂in) in from the two longest edges on the back of the striped fabric. Right sides facing, pin the striped fabric to one heart shape, aligning the raw edges. Stitch the fabrics together all around, following the pencil line. Start and finish stitching at the lowest point of the centre top of the heart.

2 Use buttons to decorate one or both of the heart shapes. Arrange the buttons into a pleasing design, then pencil the design onto the front of the fabric and sew on the buttons.

4 Right sides facing, pin the other heart to the free side of the striped fabric. Ensure that the two hearts are aligned or the pin-cushion will be twisted. Sew the fabrics together as before, leaving a small gap. Turn the pin-cushion right side out and stuff it, ensuring that the it is all well-filled. Sew up the gap with small oversewing stitches.

beaded
napkin
ring

Most of us have a collection of safety pins sitting in a drawer doing nothing. This project shows you how to combine them with beads and elastic to make an unusual napkin ring. Choose beads with a hole large enough to thread onto the pin, but not so large that they prevent the pin from closing. I have used silver and crystal beads, but you can use any colour or combination of colours you want. Turn to page 20 for more clever napkin ring ideas.

Turn to page 20 for more clever napkin ring ideas.

YOU WILL NEED

42 safety pins, each measuring 3.5cm (1³⁄₈in) long

260 silver beads and 42 crystal beads. (This quantity will vary depending on the size of beads you choose. Calculate how many you need by filling one pin and multiplying the number by 42)

Shearing elastic

Needle with an eye large enough to take the shearing elastic

1 Open each safety pin and fill the pin with beads, leaving enough space at the point to close the pin again. I filled twenty-eight pins with six silver beads and fourteen pins with three of the longer crystal beads.

3 When you have threaded on all the pins, pull the elastic up to bring all the pins together, but allowing a little flexibility for slipping the ring over a napkin. Tie the ends together tightly and trim off any excess elastic.

2 Thread the needle with shearing elastic. Take the needle through the loop at the bottom of a pin, through a silver bead, then through the bottom loop of the next pin. Make sure that the beaded pins are all facing the same way. Continue threading the pins onto the elastic, adding an extra bead between every fifth pin.

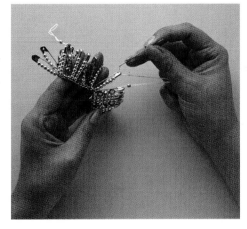

4 Thread the needle with another length of elastic and take it through the holes in the heads of the pins, adding one silver bead between each pinhead. Pull up the elastic so that this end of the ring is the same diameter as the other and tie it as before.

more ideas for napkin rings

Bring sparkling style to your dinner table with individually decorated napkin rings fashioned from broken necklaces and old bracelets.

LEFT TO RIGHT

- *Chunky glass beads threaded onto ribbon and tied around a napkin.*
- *Expandable amber-coloured bracelet slipped over a napkin.*

- *Glass and pearl necklace tied around a napkin.*
- *Pearl necklace wrapped around a napkin.*

- *Napkin ring made from glass and crystal beads threaded onto thin craft wire.*

button & braid shelf trim

Jazz up a plain wooden shelf unit with lengths of furnishing braid for texture and buttons for decoration. Choose a braid that is exactly the same width as the edges of the shelves and similar-sized buttons in complementary or contrasting colours. The same method can be used to add interest to book shelves or even kitchen cupboards.

YOU WILL NEED

Furnishing braid the length of your shelves plus a little extra for the turn

PVA glue

Buttons (number depends on size of shelves to be decorated) no wider than the thickness of the shelves

Pen

Panel pins

Small hammer

1 Take a length of braid and lay it along the longest edge of the shelf unit, without stretching it. Cut it exactly to length. Squeeze out a line of glue along the centre of the edge and lay the braid in place. Leave it to dry for ten minutes.

3 Arrange the buttons on the tape. Ensure that there is one over every point where two lengths of tape meet to help keep the ends in place. When you are happy with the arrangement, make a tiny pen mark under each button.

2 Lay a length of braid along an adjacent edge of the unit and cut it to length, but this time allow an extra 2cm (³⁄₄in) so that you can double over the ends to make neat edges. Cover all the shelf edges in this way, leaving each piece of braid to dry for ten minutes before starting the next one.

4 Nail the buttons in place one by one. For a really neat look, make sure that the holes in the buttons are all at the same angle, parallel to the shelf edges.

buttoned cuffs & cushion

Pearl buttons have a quality all of their own. Their lustre catches the light, while the weight of them and their coarse reverse side, distinguishes them from plastic imitations. Use them to great effect on shirt cuffs or turn a monogrammed napkin into a cushion and decorate it with your finest 'pearlers'.

YOU WILL NEED

For a shirt:

Plain shirt (I used one with double cuffs, but normal cuffs work just well)

Approximately 200 buttons

Needle

White thread

Scissors

For a cushion:

Monogrammed napkin

10 large pearl buttons

Needle

White thread

Scissors

Stuffing

CUFFS

1 This project works best if all the buttons are a similar colour, although they can be different sizes, shapes and patterns. If you follow this guideline, the different buttons will look very striking when mixed together.

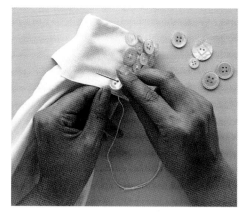

2 Starting on one short edge, work up and down in rows across the cuff until it is completely covered with buttons. Check that each button sits neatly in place before stitching it firmly to the fabric.

CUSHION

1 Fold the napkin in half and position five buttons down each short side. Stitch them firmly in place. If the edges of the napkin are plain, machine around the open sides, right sides facing, leaving a small gap. Turn right side out. If the edges are shaped, hand-stitch round the open sides with tiny slip or oversewing stitches, wrong sides facing, leaving a small gap.

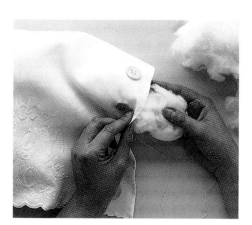

2 It is best to use synthetic wadding to stuff the cushion as it can then be washed by hand if it gets dirty. Fill the cushion with stuffing, making sure that it is evenly distributed and reaches into all the corners. Stitch up the gap by hand.

tabletop christmas tree

This centrepiece for the festive table can be made in minutes and lasts all holiday. It takes up little space and would also work well on a mantelpiece or window ledge. Strings of pearls stand in for traditional tinsel and the branches are laden with pearly earrings instead of glass baubles.

YOU WILL NEED

Small tree in a pot

Piece of fabric the circumference of the pot plus 5cm (2in) and the height of the pot plus 6cm (2½in)

Masking tape

Double-sided sticky tape

Gold ribbon

1 handful of glass nuggets

1 handful of marbles

Some loose pearls

Light-weight strings of beads (broken necklaces are ideal)

Earrings (odd ones are fine for this project)

1 Masking tape one end of the fabric to the pot and wrap it around the pot. Fold in the raw edge of the other end of the fabric and stick it over the masking tape with double-sided tape. Tuck 4cm (1½in) of fabric into the top of the pot. Tuck 2cm (¾in) under the pot and tape it in place.

2 Fill around the top of the pot with glass nuggets, marbles and pearls. Tie gold ribbon in a bow around the pot (*see inset*) and add a clip-on earring to its knot.

3 Wind strings of beads around the tree, putting the heavier ones close to the trunk and the lighter ones on the ends of the branches.

4 Either clip or hook (depending on the original fixing) a selection of different earrings to the branches of the tree.

two button picture frames

You can use buttons inside and outside picture frames. Glued around a shadow frame they add colour and texture. Alternatively, fill the frame with buttons for a neat way of displaying and storing them. You can complete the effect by making a button picture, too.

YOU WILL NEED

For a glued frame:

Shadow frame

Enough buttons to cover the frame

PVA glue

Small buttons in a contrasting colour

For a filled frame:

Shadow frame

Piece of cream coloured sugar paper

Small buttons

PVA glue

Furnishing braid

Clear sticky tape

Enough buttons to completely fill the inside of the frame

GLUED FRAME

1 Put a blob of glue on the back of each button and stick it to the frame. Do not use too much glue or it will seep through the buttonholes when you stick it down.

2 Use contrasting-coloured buttons to make a picture in the box section of the frame. Stick the picture in position with dabs of glue, then assemble the frame.

FILLED FRAME

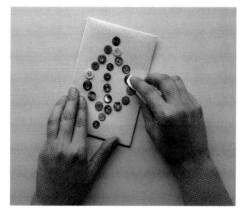

1 Using small buttons and PVA glue, make a picture on the sugar paper; use a tissue to wipe away any glue that seeps through the buttonholes. Make a border from braid.

2 Stick the design to the back of the glass with tiny pieces of clear sticky tape. Fill the inside of the frame with buttons, making sure that as many as possible face forwards. Mix colours, sizes and patterns, then replace the back of the frame.

beaded christmas star

This easy-to-make and decorate Christmas star can be hung on the tree, in a window, or strung from a garland. It is the perfect project for recycling broken necklaces and collections of odd beads. Make as many as you have the materials for; they look stunning together. Turn to page 32 for more star ideas.

YOU WILL NEED

5 wooden satay skewers, 15cm (6in) long

Fine gold-coloured craft wire

Gold spray

Beads

1 Arrange the wooden skewers into the shape of a five-pointed star. Some skewers will lie over others and the ends should just overlap one another.

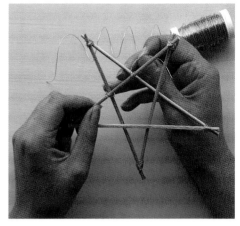

2 Using 10cm (4in) lengths of wire, bind the ends of the skewers together to make the star. Then, bind the skewers together where they overlap. Spray the star gold and leave it to dry.

3 Thread a bead onto the end of a 30cm (12in) piece of wire and twist the wire over the bead to stop it, and subsequent beads, falling off. Loosely fill the wire with beads, leaving gaps to allow the wire to wrap around the star.

4 Starting at one point, wrap the beaded wire right over an arm of the star. Take the wire across to the next arm and wrap it up and then back down the arm. Continue in this way until all the arms are wrapped. If you run out of wire, just secure the end round a skewer and continue with a new beaded length.

more ideas for christmas stars

Different beads give very different effects and the skewers can be thickly or thinly covered for a chunky or more fragile look.

LEFT TO RIGHT
• *Pearl star*
• *Agate-coloured beaded star*
• *Crystal beads make a glittering star*
• *Mixed bead star*
• *Use shiny beads for a pretty pink star*

buttons & beads

button & rose heart

Buttons saved from baby's and children's clothes can be turned into a delicate heart to commemorate a wedding or Christening in the next generation. After the big day the heart can be displayed in a shadow box.

YOU WILL NEED

100cm (40in) of 1cm- (¹/₂in-) wide pale blue ribbon

150 4cm- (1¹/₂in-) long pearl-headed pins

14cm- (5¹/₂in-) long polystyrene heart base

13 silk roses in three colours

100g (4oz) box of standard pins

150 pearly buttons

150 small blue beads

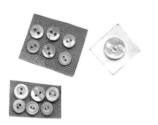

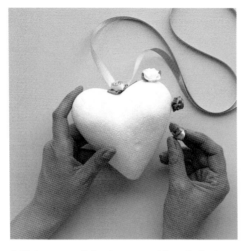

1 Using two of the long pearl-headed pins, attach the ribbon to the top of the heart. Push a standard pin through the centre of a silk rose and press the pin into the edge of the heart. Pin alternate-coloured roses all around the edge of the heart shape.

2 With standard pins, attach a row of pearl beads around the edge of the heart. Add two more rows of beads. Pin three different-coloured roses to the centre.

3 Pin the buttons to the heart with pearl-headed pins. Start next to the rows of beads and work right round the heart then in towards the centre. Take time to arrange them to fill the gaps as much as possible.

4 Using standard pins, pin small blue beads into any gaps that are left. Turn over the heart and repeat steps 2-4 on the other side.

buttons & beads

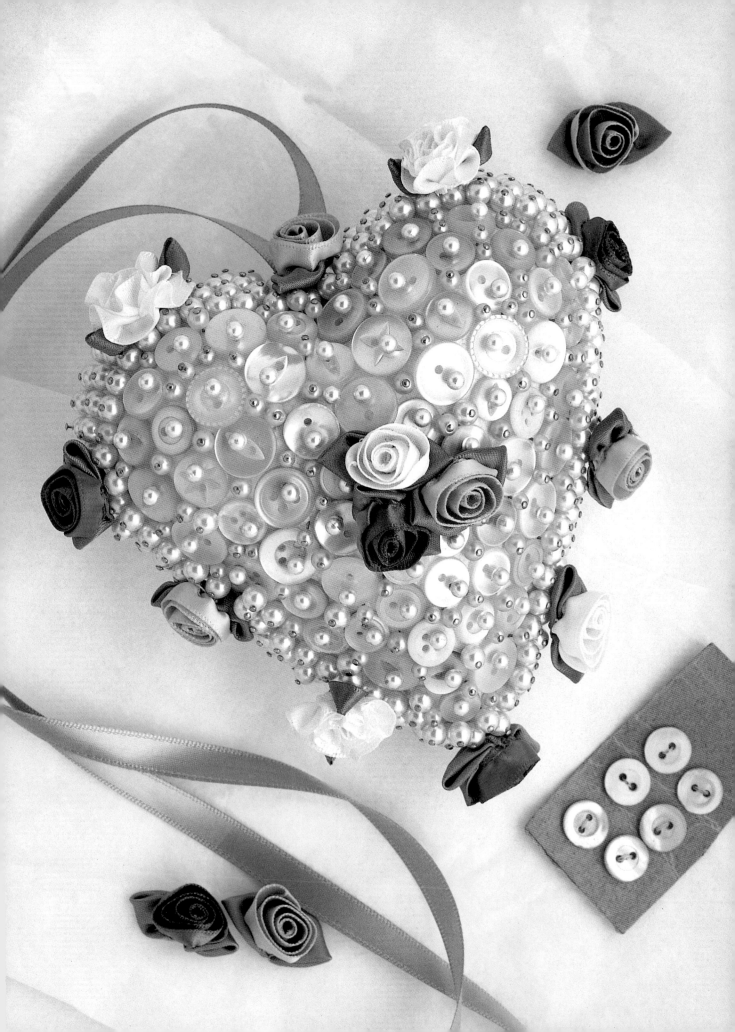

papers & stamps

There are so many wonderful papers to choose from these days. There are lovely hand-made papers, recycled papers, bits of colourful tissue and foil sweet wrappers, old manuscripts and stamps from all around the world. Stamps are beautiful, each one of them a tiny work of art in its own right. They are ideal design materials and lend themselves very well to the surface decoration of boxes. Arranged in themes of colour, subject or country of origin, they give a stunning effect. Tell your friends that you are collecting stamps and in no time at all they will come flooding in.

LEFT *Holiday memory box, page 52.*
TOP *Greetings card, page 46.*
ABOVE *Wallpaper envelopes, page 50.*
RIGHT *Butterfly-stamp display box, page 44.*

stamp finger plates

Protect your doors from sticky hands by adding old-fashioned glass finger plates. However, you can make them both contemporary and individual by decorating them with stamps and adding gold details. I used stamps with botanical and piscine pictures for a natural theme. You can use exactly the same technique to decorate larger items, such as a glass table top, although you will need a lot of stamps for this!

YOU WILL NEED

Glass finger plate

Stamps

Wallpaper paste

Small paintbrush

Gold size

Gold leaf

Vine template, page 124

Large paintbrush

Dark card

Pencil

Scissors

Two small brass screws

1 If the stamps are attached to envelopes soak in water for a few minutes to detach them. Check them every minute or so as they can become soggy if left for too long. Use wallpaper paste to stick the stamps face down onto the back of the finger plate. Leave them to dry.

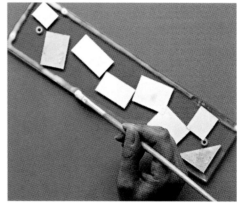

2 Using the fine paintbrush, paint a free-hand border of gold size around the edge of the finger plate.

3 When the gold size becomes clear and tacky, place a piece of gold leaf over it. Rub the paper backing to ensure that the leaf is stuck down then peel the paper off. Brush off the surplus leaf with the large brush. Lay the vine template face up under the face down finger plate, so that you can see the design through the glass. Paint over it with gold size and add gold leaf as described.

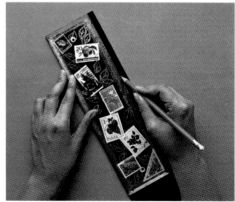

4 When all the gold leaf is dry, lay the finger plate on the dark card. Draw around the edge then cut out the card. When you screw the finger plate to the door, screw through the card at the same time to hold it in place.

paper roses

Celebrate the loveliest of all our flowers by making these everlasting blooms from crepe paper. Fill a vase with your crop or make a bunch for a friend in their favourite colour and tie the stems with a pretty ribbon.

YOU WILL NEED

For each flower:

6cm (2¹/₂in) strip of crepe paper

Scissors

Wire coat hanger

Wire cutters

Florist's tape

1 Fold a right-angled triangle in one end of the crepe paper by taking the strip down over itself. Fold another triangle next to it, again taking the paper over itself. Make two more triangles in the same way and you will have a complete square. Continue folding in the same way, making more squares on top of the first one (*see inset*) until you reach the end of the strip of paper.

2 Holding the layers of paper together with one hand, push the very end of the strip down through the hole in the middle. This is easier if you first twist the end of the paper around to make it both narrower and stiffer.

3 Still holding the layers together, grasp the poked-through end at the back of the layers and twist it firmly in clockwise direction. The layers of paper on the top will start to stand up and form petals, which you can encourage by gently twisting them anti-clockwise. Do not pull on the end of the paper or the petals will disappear through the centre of the rose.

4 When all the petals are formed, tape the poked-through end and the free end at the base of the flower together with florist's tape. Cut a length of wire from a coat hanger and tape it to the paper ends. Wind florist's tape round the ends several times to create a bulbous base for the rose. Wind the tape down the wire, slightly over-lapping each turn to cover the whole stem. Cut off any excess tape.

parcel
wrap
vase

A lot of paper is used in packaging and posting and I've ripped many a parcel open and wished there was a good way of recycling the brown wrapping paper. So, I came up with this stylish, post-marked vase, a perfect way of using paper and of giving a new lease of life to an old or ugly vase. I filled my vase with the paper flowers shown in the previous project.

YOU WILL NEED

A vase

Wallpaper paste

Brown wrapping paper

Postcard or letter with an interesting postmark

Soft pencil

Masking tape

Dark brown paint

Fine paintbrush

Eraser

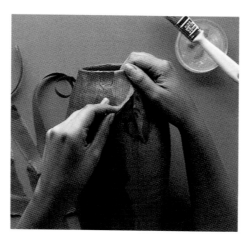

1 Tear strips of parcel wrap and paste it onto the vase with wallpaper paste. Work from just inside the top edge of the vase, down its length and across the base.

3 Tape the photocopy in position on the vase, right side out. Sharpen the pencil and carefully draw over the photocopied postmark, thus transferring the graphite on the back of the paper onto the vase.

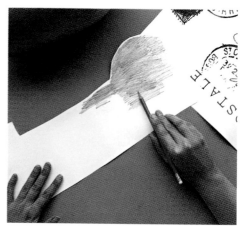

2 Enlarge the postmark on a photocopier until it will cover a good proportion of the vase. The edge of the postmark may 'break up', which will add to the finished look. With a soft pencil, cover the back of the photocopy with graphite.

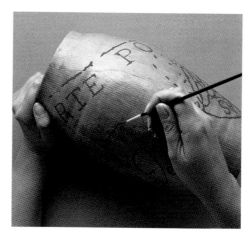

4 Carefully peel the photocopy off the vase. With the fine brush, paint over the graphite lines to reproduce the postmark. Use an eraser to remove any surplus graphite. Leave the paint to dry then seal the paper with three coats of matt varnish. The vase is now splash-proof, but it shouldn't be immersed in water.

butterfly-stamp display box

Hold a beautiful collection of butterflies captive with this little box project. In years gone by people would kill butterflies in order to pin them into their collections, but use stamps instead and not a single butterfly has to die for this philatelic display.

YOU WILL NEED

Box, an old cigar box is ideal

Emulsion paint

Paintbrush

6 stamps

Foam board

Paper

Pencil

Metal rule

Craft knife

Cutting mat

Glue

Pins with coloured heads

1 Paint the box inside and out with two coats of paint to give an even, solid colour. Leave it to dry.

3 Cut a piece of foam board to fit inside the box and lay it in place. Cut a piece of paper to the same size and lay that on top of the foam board. Lay each stamp in turn on a piece of foam board and draw round it. Cut out the piece of foam board 2mm (¹/₈in) inside the drawn lines.

2 If any of the stamps are attached to envelopes, soak them in water for a couple of minutes to detach them. However, do keep a check on them, as they can soon become too soggy.

4 Glue the stamps to the pieces of foam board. Arrange the stamps inside the box and pin them in place.

papers & stamps

greetings card

This colourful and exotic card is really simple to make and provides the perfect opportunity for using up all sorts of bits and pieces. I have used sweet wrappers and ethnic mirrors, but you can use many other decorations, see pages 48-49 for more ideas. Do bear in mind that the decoration musn't be too heavy, or the card won't stand up.

see pages 48-49 for more ideas.

YOU WILL NEED

Rectangles of coloured craft paper

Foil sweet papers with coloured designs

Paper glue

Tiny mirrors with embroidered surrounds

Scissors

Thin tinsel

If you wish to make envelopes for these cards, use pieces of coloured craft paper and follow the instructions for the wallpaper envelope *project on page 50.*

follow the instructions for the wallpaper envelope project on page 50.

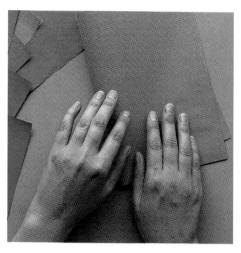

1 Fold the craft paper widthways and then lengthways to make a double-skinned card. This will make the paper strong enough to stand up on its own.

2 Carefully flatten out a foil sweet wrapper and glue it to the centre of the card using paper glue.

3 Glue a tiny mirror to the centre of the design on the foil wrapper. These mirrors can be salvaged from 1970s dresses or ethnic clothing or bought on rolls from ethnic haberdashery shops.

4 Cut short lengths of tinsel, curl them up and glue them to the corners of the foil. Tinsel often has wire through the centre, so don't cut it with your best scissors.

more ideas for greetings cards

Hand-made cards are lovely both to give and receive, and these are so quick to make that there really are no more excuses for buying ready-made ones. Glass nuggets may not survive the postal system, so only use them on cards you can deliver by hand.

LEFT TO RIGHT
- *Two colours of craft paper decorated with green glass nugget and sequins.*
- *Card bordered with foil tape, with sequins and an antique glass decoration.*

- *Pinked strips of foil paper and a recycled paper Christmas tree with sequin baubles.*
- *Pinked stars decorated with flat glass nuggets. The top layer of sugar paper has*

been torn to expose a different coloured under-layer down one side.
- *A piece of curled-up tinsel glued to the centre of a foil sweet wrapper, inside a block of pinked foil paper.*

- *A foil sweet wrapper with an ethnic mirrored decoration and rows of coloured sequins.*

papers & stamps

wallpaper envelopes

Offcuts of wallpaper can be recycled to make pretty envelopes that will brighten anyone's day. Use papers with small floral or checkered patterns that suit the scale of an envelope and make sure that they do not have a pre-pasted back, or if they get damp your letter will be sealed inside for ever. An old but elegantly shaped toast rack doubles as an ideal letter holder.

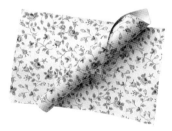

YOU WILL NEED

Envelope template, page 125 or an old envelope the size and shape you require

Offcuts of various wallpapers

Pencil

Scissors

Ruler

Double-sided sticky tape

1 If you are using the template on page 125, enlarge it to the size you require on a photocopier, then cut it out. If you are copying an old envelope, open it out carefully to avoid tearing it. This will be the template for your wallpaper envelope.

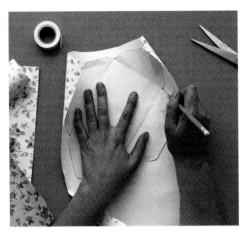

2 Using a pencil, draw around the template onto the back of the wallpaper. Make dots at the edges of the fold lines to indicate where they will go.

3 Carefully cut out the wallpaper envelope. Use sharp scissors or a craft knife and cutting mat to cut along the lines. It is important that you cut out the shape neatly, as wobbly edges will make the finished envelope look tatty.

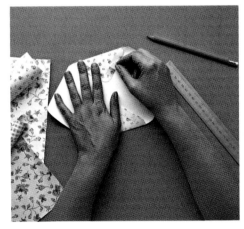

4 Keeping the template next to you as a guide, fold up the wallpaper envelope, using a ruler to fold the flaps against. Stick a small piece of double-sided sticky tape to each of the side flaps at the point where the base flap will fold up to meet them. Peel the backing off the tape and stick the envelope together. Use double-sided tape to seal the top flap, but remember to put your letter in the envelope first.

holiday memory box

Coming back from abroad, I find I have pockets full of such things as tram tickets and postcards that I've collected as I've moved around. Here is a project to make a box file for holiday photographs, decorated with travel memorabilia.

Or, on a more practical level, store travel documents in it and find your passport in record time, plus your tickets, visas and any unused currency.

YOU WILL NEED

Box with a deep lid

Emulsion paint

Postcards (I used old ones, but you could use modern ones)

Photographs

Glue

Foreign currency

Selection of coloured card

Scissors

1 Paint the box inside and out with two coats of paint to give an even, solid colour. Leave it to dry.

3 When you are happy with the arrangement, glue the cards in place. You can stick pictures across the opening, but remember to carefully cut them through before opening the box.

2 Arrange postcards and photographs on one side of the box. Handwriting on a card can be as decorative as the picture.

4 Place heavy books on the cards to weigh them down and leave them to dry flat. Repeat the process on the other visible sides of the box. Embellish the box further by gluing on any foreign coins or other travel memorabilia. Make dividers from coloured card to fit the box.

metal &
wire

I love all metals from bright shiny chrome to weathered rusty iron: they each have a unique quality. Don't be afraid to mix different metals together; for example, I think silver- and gold-coloured metals look particularly good combined in a project. However, when working with metal of any kind, do be careful as the edges are often sharp. Wear gloves and make sure that everything is out of a child's reach. You can also buy metallic paints and sprays, metal leaf and gilding creams to use in projects. From glamorous gold leaf to humble baked-bean cans, here are some creative results from some unlikely junk items.

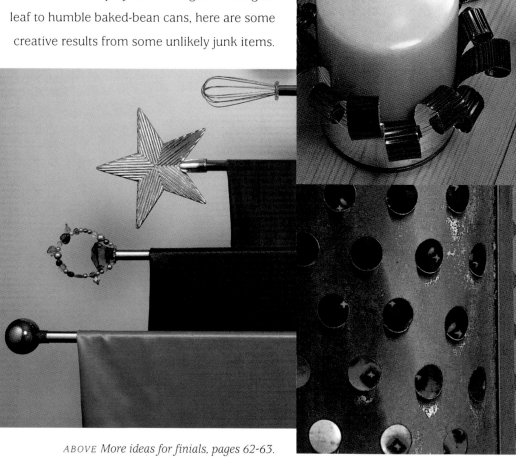

ABOVE More ideas for finials, pages 62-63.

LEFT Cheese grater candle sconce, page 56. ABOVE Tin-can candle holders, page 66. RIGHT Copper wreath with tin leaves, page 58.

cheese grater candle sconce

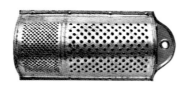

Here's a cunning idea: turn an old metal cheese grater into a sconce. As night descends, the flickering light will bring a warm glow and cosy atmosphere to your room. The half-moon shaped graters are ideal as they already have a hole in the top for hanging. Alternatively, simply place a candle inside a large round grater.

YOU WILL NEED

Metal cheese grater

Piece of thin metal sheet big enough to easily cover the base of the grater and strong enough to take the weight of the candle

Marker pen

Metal cutters

Glue gun or strong glue

Candle

1 Stand the cheese grater on the thin metal sheet and draw around the base of it with the marker pen.

3 Cut out the whole drawn shape. Then, carefully cut between each of the 'teeth', up to the original outline of the base of the cheese grater. Bend each of the metal 'teeth' upwards, at right angles to the base section.

2 Add a row of 'teeth' along the curved and the straight edges, but not at the corner points, of the base shape.

4 Run glue along the outside of the curved edge of the 'teeth' and press these inside the curved edge of the grater. Do this carefully as the glue gun gets hot. Leave to dry. Glue along the outside back edge of the grater and press the straight row of 'teeth' against it.
Put a candle inside the grater and light it carefully. Remember never to leave a lighted candle in a draft or unattended.

copper wreath with tin leaves

This contemporary and very stylish Christmas wreath is in fact made from recycled electrical cable and old tin cans. Display it indoors and it will catch and reflect the light: hang it outside and some of the leaves will rust to a golden colour and then to brown, just like real leaves.

YOU WILL NEED

4m (156in) copper wire. You can strip the plastic covering off old electrical cable, or buy new wire

Rolling pin or the cardboard tube from inside a roll of kitchen paper

1m (39in) fine craft wire

Four tin cans

Can opener

Protective gloves

Tin snips

Leaf template, page 125

Marker pen

Small pliers

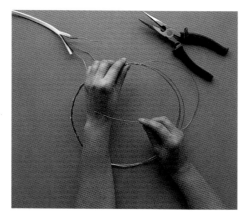

1 Make a circle of copper wire the size of an average dinner plate. Take the wire round twice more to make a strong, triple circle. Then wind more wire over all three strands of wire, right around the circle to hold it together.

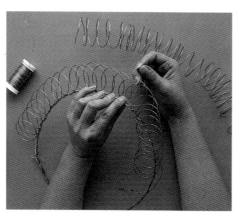

3 Flatten the spring sideways right along its length. Using the fine craft wire, attach the flattened spring to the copper wire circle. Take the craft wire through each coil of the copper spring, around the wire circle and through the next coil. Continue in this way until the whole spring is attached to the circle. Snip off any excess coils of spring.

2 Coil the remaining copper wire neatly around a rolling pin or a cardboard tube so that it looks like a spring. When you have coiled all the wire, slide it off the rolling pin.

4 Cut both ends off the tin cans with a can opener. Wearing protective gloves, cut along the seam of the cans with tin snips, then flatten the cans out. Cut out the leaf template and draw around it onto the tin can with a marker pen. Cut out the leaves and rub off any surplus marker pen. Attach the leaves to the wreath at regular intervals by bending the stem over the copper circle with small pliers.

wire curtain pole finial

Spin a spider's web of wire to make an intriguing finial; add it to a chrome wardrobe pole and you can create a designer look at a fraction of the price. Once you have made one you will want to adorn all the windows in your home in a unique and creative manner, so turn to page 62 for more ideas.

YOU WILL NEED

Wire that is flexible but firm

Pliers

Reel of fine florist's or craft wire

Chrome wardrobe pole slightly longer than the width of your chosen window

1 Cut a 50cm (20in) length of the thicker wire. Make a loop about the size of a large avocado, leaving the ends free to be pushed inside the pole. Make a second, slightly larger loop, and place it to bisect the first loop. Twist the bottom of the loops together.

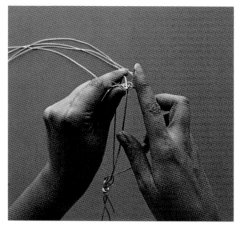

2 Where the loops cross at the top, bind them together with the fine wire until it feels secure.

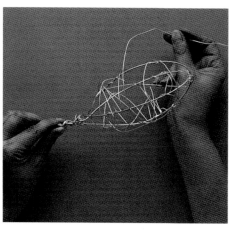

3 Straighten ends of the wire shape so there is something to hold while you construct the next stage. Now, taking lengths of fine wire, weave them around the loops until the whole shape is covered with a network of wire.

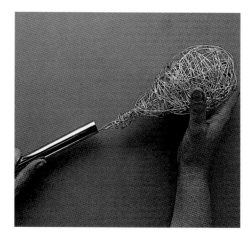

4 Bind the ends of the loop together with fine wire and wind more wire around them until they fit snugly into the pole. The finial should not fall out unless you pull it quite hard. You can make a small coil of wire to sit around the end of the pole as an extra detail if you wish.

more ideas for finials

If the previous project inspired you, here are a few more ideas for decorating your windows. All of them are easy to make and will add a stylish detail to the most ordinary window.

LEFT TO RIGHT

• *A Christmas tree bauble with a collar made from a foil sweet wrapper where it meets the pole.*

• *Screw a door handle into a bottle cork and push that into the pole. Decorate the finial further with a ring of wired beads.*

• *A Christmas tree star finds a new use.*

• *A whisk fitted into a pole makes an ideal finial for a kitchen window.*

• *Pinecone sprayed gold and mounted on a 5cm (2in)screw. Cover the screw with masking tape until it fits the pole.*

wire plant support

Twist and turn wire to make bird-shaped plant supports. Ivy or other climbing plants will grow around and up the birds, giving them leaves for feathers. Once the nailed outline has been made you can make flocks of birds quite speedily to give to family and friends.

YOU WILL NEED

Piece of wood

Bird template, page 126

Marker pen

Hammer

23 nails

100cm (39in) of thick wire

Pliers

Fine florist's wire

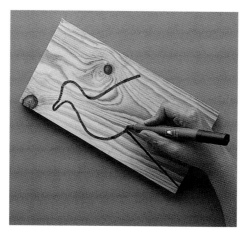

1 Enlarge the template to the required size and draw around it onto the piece of wood. Go over the lines with marker pen so that you can see them easily.

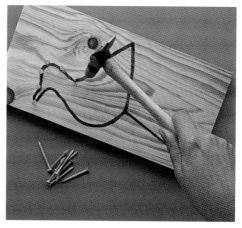

2 Hammer the nails into the wood, following the lines, every 1.5cm (⅝in). Where there are any curves, hammer in nails more frequently.

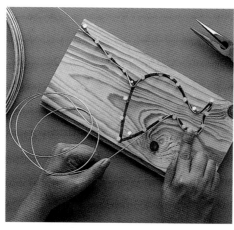

3 Starting 30cm (12in) from one end of the wire (this free 30cm [12in] length makes the stalk), curve the wire in and out of the nails right around the bird shape. Lift the wire off the nails and twist any excess around the stalk.

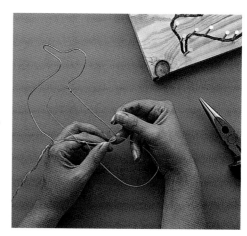

4 Using the fine wire, make a curve for the bird's wing and then the tail, joining each end to the thicker wire by bending it around with the pliers.

tin-can candle holders

Turn ordinary tin cans into stylish candle and plant holders. They not only look great, as their shinning exteriors sparkle in the candlelight, but they also keep the candle wax from spilling. Large catering cans make ideal planters for spring bulbs to complement your candles. Be careful when doing this project, as the cut can edges are very sharp.

YOU WILL NEED

Empty tin cans

Can opener that takes the rim as well as the lid fully off

Marker pen

Ruler

Tin snips

Round nose pliers

Protective gloves

The plant holder is made from a catering-size can with the edge cut into scallops with tin snips. This method was also used to make the candle holders with petal edges.

1 Wash the tin cans and use the opener to take the top rims off if they are still in place. With the pen, mark vertical lines down the can at regular intervals.

2 Wearing protective gloves, cut down the marked lines with the tin snips. Do not cut right to the base of the can. Vary the widths of the strips on different cans for thinner or fatter curls.

3 Grasp the top of each strip with the pliers and curl it over, down to the bottom of the cut line. You need to curl the strips quite tightly, as they will spring back a little.

4 Continue working around the can until all the strips are curled. If necessary, you can adjust the curls afterwards so that they are all at an even height.
Put a candle or nightlight inside the holder. Remember never to leave a lighted candle in a draft or unattended.

colander hanging baskets

Give old enamelware a new lease of life, and bring colour into your garden at the same time, by converting colanders into hanging baskets. This is such a simple project to do and the results are both pretty and good for your plants, as colanders provide ideal drainage.

YOU WILL NEED

Two enamel colanders of different sizes

Three 30cm (12in) lengths of galvanized chain (each length must have exactly the same number of links)

Three 50cm (20in) lengths of galvanized chain (each length must have exactly the same number of links)

Seven bolts, each measuring 1.5cm (⅝in) long, with nuts to fit. The bolts must be narrow enough to fit through the holes in the colander and the rings of the chain.

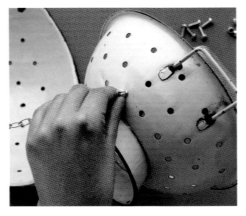

1 Divide the circumference of the lowest row of holes in the small colander approximately into three and mark the nearest hole. Bolt one end of each 30cm (12in) length of chain to the outside of the colander through each marked hole. Push the bolt through from the outside and loosely screw on the nut from the inside.

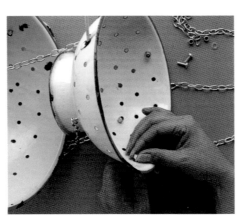

3 On the smaller colander, mark the holes in the top row that are directly above the bolted holes in the bottom row. Bolt one end of each 50cm (20in) length of chain to these marked holes.

2 Sit the small colander inside the large one and align the handles. On the large colander, mark the hole in the top row that is nearest in line to the bolted holes in the smaller colander. Bolt the other ends of the 30cm (12in) lengths of chain to these marked holes in the same way as before.

4 Link the other ends of the 50cm (20in) lengths of chain together with the remaining bolt. Hang the colanders up from the joined chain and check that they are balanced and hang evenly before tightening up all the bolts.

more ideas for plant containers Used outdoors, these metal planters make unusual plant holders in the garden. Colanders provide perfect drainage, but you will have to drill holes in the base of the other containers.

metal & wire

LEFT TO RIGHT
- *White enamelled mug holding a pink cyclamen.*
- *Kitchen colander planted with heather.*
- *Rusty tin with a hebe plant.*
- *Enamelled container holding heather.*
- *Enamelled tea pot filled with cyclamen.*
- *Colander planted with a fern.*

metal & wire

fabrics & ribbons

I have more than one blanket box that is filled to overflowing with fabrics of all kinds: bargain-bin impulse buys, intricately knitted old woollen jumpers, kilts and scarves, ribbons salvaged from wrapped gifts and scraps of trimmings left over from larger projects. Outgrown and outdated clothes made from good-quality and attractively coloured or patterned fabrics are ideal for many projects. If you do not have exactly the right piece for fabric for a project, comb your local second-hand clothes shop. Ignore styles, look just for colours and patterns. It is better to buy all-natural fabrics such as wool, cotton, linen or silk as they tend to wear better than synthetic fabrics. Such clothes are also a good source of buttons, which can be used for projects in the *Buttons & beads* chapter.

LEFT Hot-water bottle cover, page 84.
ABOVE Appliquéd peg-bag, page 78.
RIGHT Woollen cushion, page 80.

ABOVE Perfectly wrapped presents, page 74.

perfectly wrapped presents

Learn the simple skill of perfect gift-wrapping. Stores have offered a professional gift-wrapping service for years, but it is very easily achievable at home. If your gift is an odd shape, find a suitably sized box for it: this will be much easier to wrap. Hide the sticky tape inside the wrapping paper and use glass nuggets and scraps of fancy ribbons to decorate your gifts.

YOU WILL NEED

Coloured paper

Double-sided sticky tape

Fancy ribbon

Glass nuggets

Glue

1 The paper should be large enough to wrap round the gift, plus 3cm (1¼in). At each end, allow two-thirds of the depth of the gift for the flaps. Fold under 2cm (¾in) on one side of the paper and stick a length of double-sided tape to it. Lay the paper on the gift and stick another length of tape to the right side. Remove the paper backing of the tape and fold over then stick the wrapping paper in place.

3 Stick a 3cm (1¼in) length of double-sided tape to the reverse side of the ribbon and attach it to the centre back of the gift. Wrap the ribbon around the gift and secure it to itself with another 3cm-(1¼in-) long length of tape stuck to the back of the ribbon.

2 To close the ends of the parcel, carefully fold the two outer edges of the paper flaps inwards. Do not commit yourself to making creases until you are satisfied that the folds are symmetrical. Stick a length of double-sided tape to the open end of the paper. Neatly fold and crease the open end upwards and stick it in place. Repeat the procedure at the opposite end.

4 Glue glass nuggets at regular intervals to the ribbon. If you have used ribbon with its own decoration, such as tiny mirrors, it is not necessary to add nuggets.

fabrics & ribbons

tartan ribbon heart

Short pieces of mismatched tartan ribbon were used to make this decorative heart, which can be hung up at Christmas as an alternative to a wreath. The fact that the ribbon is of varying patterns and is joined with knots adds to its charm. Sprigs of holly made from felt with bead berries give it a festive feel.

YOU WILL NEED

Wire coat hanger

Bubble wrap

Sticky tape

Lengths of tartan ribbon

Holly leaf template, page 125

Scissors

Green felt

10 large red beads

10 long pins

1 Bend the wire coat hanger into a heart shape, using the hook at the top to make a loop. Wind strips of bubble wrap thickly round the wire, taping them in place, until the whole heart is covered. Wind a thin layer of bubble wrap around the hook loop.

3 Photocopy or trace off the holly leaf template and draw around it onto green felt. Cut out about twenty leaves. Alternatively, fold a piece of paper in half and draw half a holly shape on to it. Cut this out and open it up to make your own leaf template.

2 Starting with the loop, wind a length of ribbon around the shape, slightly overlapping it on each turn to cover the bubble wrap. When you come to the end of a length of ribbon, simply tie on a new one and carry on wrapping around the heart until all the bubble wrap is covered.

4 Thread a red bead onto a pin and then pin two leaves to the heart. Pin pairs or single leaves all around the heart at random intervals. As the pins can be pulled out, this decoration must be hung out of the reach of small children.

appliquèd peg-bag

This easy-to-make peg-bag provides a pretty and practical way to keep your clothes-pegs in order. Made from a recycled denim dress and decorated with old, hand-embroidered coasters, it only requires the simplest sewing skills. While pegging out washing, hook the peg-bag onto the washing line and even on the breeziest of days it will stay handy.

YOU WILL NEED

Rectangle of denim measuring 86 x 40cm (34 x 16in)

Rectangle of ticking measuring 86 x 40cm (34 x 16in)

Pins

Needle

Thread

Brass eyelet

Hammer

Drill

Piece of bamboo 32cm (13in) long

Coat-hanger hook

Decorative coasters

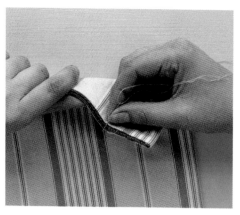

1 Right sides facing, pin the pieces of ticking and denim together. Taking a 2cm (³⁄₄in) seam allowance, stitch the fabrics together, leaving a gap in one short end. Turn right side out, stitch the gap closed and press.

3 Drill a hole halfway along the piece of bamboo and screw in the coat-hanger hook into it. Push the hook through the eyelet. Fold the fabric up so that the top edge of the denim front lies 6cm (2¹⁄₂in) below the bamboo. Lay the coasters on the front of the peg bag in a diamond pattern, then pin and sew them in place.

2 On the ticking side and at the opposite end to the sewn-up gap, measure 8cm (3in) down from the top and mark with a small pencil cross halfway across the width of the flap. Following the manufacturer's instructions, insert an eyelet at the marked spot.

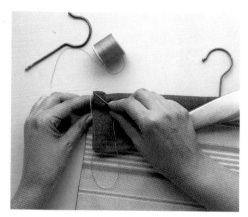

4 Stitch up 2.5cm (1in) of each end of the folded flap to hold the bamboo in place. Then, stitch up the two sides of the bag with small oversewing stitches and turn it right side out. Stitch small strips of Velcro to the underside of the flap and the corresponding point on the front of the bag to keep it closed.

woollen
cushion

Don't throw away your favourite sweater once the elbows have started to wear through, grab the scissors, remove the sleeves, add some tassels and you can turn your sweater into a bright and cheerful cushion. Alternatively, second-hand clothes shops are usually full of rails of sweaters waiting for new homes. Wash the sweater in hot water to pre-shrink it before you start.

YOU WILL NEED

Woollen sweater

Cushion pad

Scissors

Pins

Needle

Thread

Piece of card measuring 14 x 10cm (5½ x 4in)

Yarn

Darning needle

1 Lay the cushion pad on top of the sweater and, allowing 4cm (1½in) all round, cut through both the front and back to make two cushion squares.

3 Cut a slit on each side on the bottom edge of the card to hold the ends of the yarn. I made these tassels from different coloured yarns, but you can make them in a single colour. Wind each colour around the card ten times. After you have wound two colours, thread a 30cm (12in) length of yarn across the top of the card, under all the layers. Continue winding until the bundle of yarn is good and fat. Tie the length of underlying yarn tightly round the top of the bundle. Cut through all the layers of yarn at the other end (*see inset*).

2 Right sides facing, pin the two pieces together around three sides of the pad. Make sure that the pattern aligns. Remove the pad and stitch along the pinned lines. Turn right side out, re-insert the pad, then turn in raw edges and stitch the gap closed.

4 Take another 30cm (12in) piece of yarn and tie it tightly round the bundle 2.5cm (1in) down from the top of the tassel. Wrap it round six times and tie a firm knot. Thread the free ends into a darning needle and push them into the middle of the tassel. Holding all the loose ends of the tassel together, trim the bottom neatly. Stitch a tassel to each corner of the cushion.

more ideas for cushions

Turn woollen jumpers, plaid kilts and scarves into a cosy nest of cushions.

LEFT TO RIGHT, BACK TO FRONT
- *Cream plaid scarf cushion decorated with buttons.*

- *Cushion made from a Fair Isle jumper with tassels added to the corners.*

- *Kilt fabric cushion with blanket-stitched edges.*

- *Ginger-coloured cushion made from a cable-patterned sweater.*

The sleeves were unravelled and the resulting curly yarn made into tassels.

- *Cream, red and black plaid scarf made up to show the tasselled edge of the scarf.*
- *Cushion made from an intarsia sweater.*

hot-water bottle cover

As the nights draw in, warm up for winter with this cuddly hot-water bottle cover. I made this one from an old, soft woollen scarf and decorated it with a leaf motif cut from a scrap of felt

YOU WILL NEED

Scarf long enough to fold twice (not including the tasselled fringe) around the length of your hot-water bottle, by the width of the bottle plus 2cm (³⁄₄in)

Pins

Needle

Thread

Leaf motif template, page 124

Felt for motif

Yarn

1 Right sides facing, fold the scarf in half so that the tasselled ends align. Pin then stitch the two long sides together. Turn right side out.

3 Push the folded end of the scarf into the stitched, tasselled end. Push fabric inside until the ends touch, making a double-skinned bag with an open top and tasselled bottom.

2 Pin, then stitch the bottom edges together across the width of the scarf, 1cm (¹⁄₂in) above the tasselled fringe. The resulting piece of doubled fabric should be twice the length of your hot-water bottle.

4 Enlarge the template to the required size and draw around it onto the felt. Embroider veins onto the leaf and blanket stitch around it with yarn. Stitch the leaves to the front of the cover with sewing thread. Slip the hot-water bottle into the cover and tie up the top with a length of plaited yarn or a ribbon.

garden &
hedgerow

Walking and foraging in the countryside must be one of the most fulfiling ways of collecting project materials. From woodland walks to seaside paddles, the environment plays a great part when it comes to finding inspiration. Children are expert foragers, so take their lead. They often have a fascination for all things small and collectable. However, do have respect for the environment and don't be tempted to pull things from trees. Wait for them to naturally shed leaves, nuts, acorns and pieces of bark all over the woodland floor for you to squirrel away. A hollow log could be home to a family of creatures, so be selective in what you take. The same must be said of beach finds: in some countries it is illegal to take things from seashores. Some shells form natural habitats for a multitude of sea life, so do collect with common sense. All that said, have fun on your foraging trips.

LEFT Gilded book-ends, page 90.
ABOVE Twig & leaf lamp, page 92.
RIGHT More ideas for using hedgerow finds, page 94.

ABOVE Feather memo pegs, page 98.

pinecone tieback

Bring nature into your living room with these pinecone tiebacks. Turn them gold for a naturally glamorous look or leave them as they are for a rustic feel. I have hung these cones from organza ribbon, but you could substitute furnishing cord or plaited garden string.

YOU WILL NEED

For each tieback:

2 pinecones

2 brass eyelets

Gold spray

Gold cream

100cm (39in) length of ribbon

Wall hook

1 Following the instructions on the can, spray the pine cones gold, ensuring that paint gets into the crevices. Leave the cones to dry, then spray them again. Leave to dry.

2 Rub gold cream onto all outer edges of the pinecones with a cloth. Use cotton buds to rub the cream onto the inner areas.

3 Screw a brass eyelet into the end of each pinecone. These should be easy to screw in, however, if you have difficulty, make a small hole with a skewer first.

4 Thread a length of ribbon through the two eyelets. Make a simple loop at each end of the ribbon, so it can be wrapped around the curtain and the loops attached to the wall hook.

gilded bookends

Large stones are the starting blocks for these chunky bookends. They can prop up a number of books on your table top. For a large collection of books, and if you have the space, organize the books from A-Z by gilding a letter for each section. For smaller quantities of books, just gild an initial at either end of the row.

YOU WILL NEED

For each bookend:

A stone

Paper

Marker pen

Craft knife

Masking tape

Fine paintbrush

Gold size

Gold leaf

Large paintbrush

Gold-leaf sealer

1 Draw a letter onto a piece of paper. Either draw it out freehand or trace a copyright-free letter. Cut the letter out.

3 Fill in the letter with gold size and leave it to become clear and tacky. This should only take a few minutes.

2 With small pieces of masking tape, attach the letter to the stone. Trace around it with a pencil. Remove the paper letter from the stone.

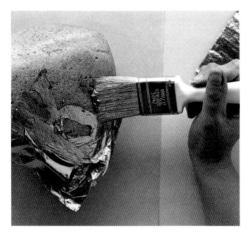

4 Place a piece of gold leaf over the sized area. Rub the paper backing to ensure that it is all stuck down then peel off the backing. Brush away any excess leaf with the large paintbrush then seal the letter with gold-leaf sealer.

twig & leaf lamp

Twigs wrapped around a lamp base and skeletal leaves added to a lampshade will bring the outdoors into the house, as well as disguising an old-fashioned base and beautifying a plain shade. This project looks almost as if the birds have neatly put it together.

YOU WILL NEED

Existing lamp base

Corrugated card

Willow twigs

Heavy-duty scissors

Rustic twine

Pale lampshade

Skeletal leaves

Paper glue

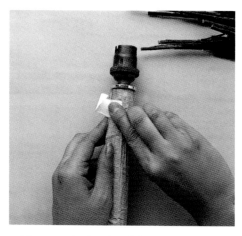

1 Measure the height of the lamp base, cut a piece of card to size and tape it around the lamp base. This gives something for the twigs to sit against and stops any of the lamp base showing through.

3 Tie the twigs tightly in place with the twine at the top, bottom and in the middle. Trim off any long bits at the top of the lamp base to neaten it.

2 Take a handful of twigs and hold them against the lamp base. Cut them slightly longer than the length of the base. Do the same with more handfuls of twigs until you have enough of the right length to surround the whole base.

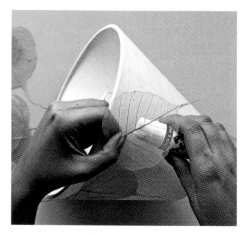

4 Apply glue thinly to the back of the skeletal leaves and stick them around the lower half of the lampshade.

more ideas for using hedgerow finds

Leaves come in all sizes shapes and colours and can be used
to decorate projects, or as decorative items in their own right.
Look out for pine cones as well, they are also versatile items.

LEFT TO RIGHT
- *Presents wrapped in textured paper and card, tied with string. Pinecones with metal eyelets (see Pinecone tiebacks, page 88) and threaded on the string.*
- *Dried leaves arranged in a picture frame*
- *Small, woodland-scented cushion, decorated with an embroidered fern motif and tiny leaf beads.*
- *Vase with a skeletal leaf spray-glued to its front.*
- *Greetings card made from oddments of paper and card and a pressed leaf.*
- *Present, as before.*

garden & hedgerow

bamboo planter

Bamboo is making a big comeback in indoor furniture, but it also looks great in the garden. You can either recycle old garden canes or lengths of bamboo can be bought reasonably cheaply in garden centres. Here is a novel way to make a planter for an actual bamboo plant, or any other shrub or tree.

YOU WILL NEED

Tea crate or packing crate measuring 35 x 35 x 40cm (14 x 14 x 16in)

26 bamboo canes, each measuring 12mm x 183cm (½ x 72in)

Measuring tape

Pencil

Small hacksaw

Sandpaper

Drill and 1mm (¹/₃₂in) drill bit

PVA wood glue

Hammer

3cm (1¼in) panel pins

Damp cloth

4 pieces of timber each measuring 5 x 1.8 x 1.8cm (2 x ¾ x ¾in)

4 pieces of timber measuring 52 x 7 x 1.8cm (20½ x 2¾ x ¾in)

45° set square

Wood filler

3cm (1¼in) paintbrush

Outdoor wood stain or paint

1 Bamboo can splinter, so take care when working with it. Cut off any splintered or damaged cane tips with the hacksaw. Measure the height of the packing crate. With a pencil mark the length onto the pieces of bamboo. Cut them to this length with the hacksaw. Sand off any rough edges.

2 Drill three holes through each piece of bamboo. Drill one hole in the centre and one hole 5cm (2in) from each end of the bamboo, the holes must be in line with each other.

3 Starting at one edge of the crate, glue and then nail a piece of bamboo into position, hammering the nails through the drilled holes to prevent the bamboo splitting. Continue gluing and nailing canes to the crate, butting them up against one another, until the whole surface is covered: small gaps are fine as they add character to the finished planter. Use a damp rag to wipe off any surplus glue.

4 Repeat the process on the other three sides of the crate. Drill holes in the base for drainage. Nail a 5cm (2in) piece of timber to each corner of the base to make feet. Cut each end of each 52cm (20½in) piece of timber to a 45° angle. Glue and nail the timber in place around the top edge of the crate (*see inset*). It should over-hang the edge of the crate by 1cm (½in) to allow rainwater to drip down without touching the bamboo. If there are any gaps, fill them with exterior wood filler and then stain or paint the timber.

feather memo pegs

These simple painted and decorated pegs make handy little memo holders. They can also hold swatches or groups of cards or mark a page in your diary or notebook in your home study. Paint them in a variety of colours and decorate them with collected feathers or imitation berries to jolly up any office.

YOU WILL NEED

Wooden pegs (the metal sprung type)

Paints

Feathers

Imitation berries

Clear-drying glue

Raffia

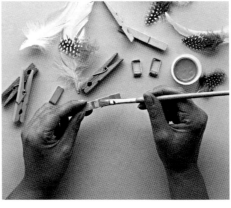

1 Detach the wooden part of the peg from its spring and paint it in your chosen colour. Leave the peg to dry then put it back together again.

2 Put a blob of clear glue onto the front of the peg and press a long feather into it. Leave the glue to dry.

3 Glue on a shorter feather in a contrasting colour. Tie a piece of raffia securely around the feather's quill. This can be a bit fiddly, so cut the raffia longer than you need, then trim the ends.

4 Alternatively, glue a sprig of imitation berries on top of the long feather and raffia. Leave to dry.

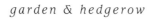

pumpkin crate

I had my eye on the fruit crates that get thrown away from the fruit stalls in our local market each week. The stall-holders were only too willing to give them away and I was sure I could find a use for them. I decided to paint and decorate a crate to hold my Halloween pumpkins, and I painted another to hold the rest of my fruit.

YOU WILL NEED

Fruit crate

Emulsion paints

Paintbrush

Templates, page 126

Balsa wood

Craft knife

Glue

1 Paint the fruit crate inside and out with two coats of paint to get an even, solid colour. Leave it to dry.

3 Cut out the pumpkin and leaf shapes with a craft knife. Paint them in vivid bold colours, using emulsion paints (*see inset*). Leave them to dry.

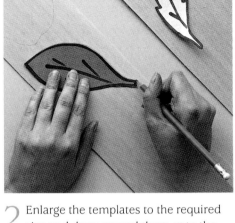

2 Enlarge the templates to the required size and draw around them onto the balsa wood. Alternatively, draw your own shapes on paper, cut them out and draw around them onto the wood.

4 Lay the crate on its side and glue some painted pumpkins and leaves to it. Lay a heavy book over each piece while it dries to keep it flat. Repeat the process on each side of the crate.

twig & pinecone star

Christmas is a time for sparkle and here's a bright and beautiful twinkling star to hang on your wall where it will catch the light. The star is decorated with small pinecones and covered with a sprinkling of glitter to look like crystallized snow and capture the essence of the season.

YOU WILL NEED

3 willow twigs

Cutters

Ruler

Fine craft wire

18 small pinecones

White paint

Glue

Glitter

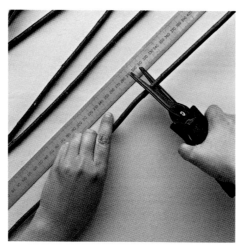

1 Measure and cut each piece of willow to 30cm (12in) long. Lay them out so that they intersect in the middle, forming a six-pointed star shape.

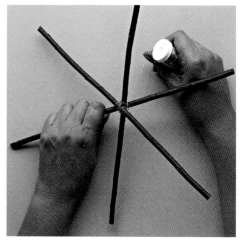

2 Wire the three twigs together in their centre. To make the star secure, weave the wire above and below each stick.

3 Twist wire around the stems of a pinecone. Do the same to two more, then wire the group of three to the end of a willow twig. Repeat the procedure on each end of each twig.

4 Paint the whole star white and leave it to dry. Cover it with glue and lay it on a piece of paper (to catch the excess glitter). Sprinkle glitter thickly over the whole star. Once the glitter is dry, you can add a bit more where it is needed.

china &
glass

I love blue and white china and have collected
many pieces over the years. At first, I was so upset
if I broke a piece, but nowadays, rather than
lamenting, I see breakages as excuses for celebra-
tion, as I can then make another mosaic project.
Chipped cups, saucers and plates are
usually left on sale stalls long after everything
else has been sold and can often be picked
up as a job lot bargain. As they are already
damaged, you can break them up with a light
heart. Don't worry that you have a harlequin
set of pieces, just try and find a common
denominator. Colour is a good enough visual
link, or floral motifs work well together.
Glass nuggets are a relatively recent invention
and can be put to all manner of uses, as can
chunky glass beads that refract the light. Look for
sea-washed glass, or 'mermaid's tears' as they
are often known, when walking on the beach.

ABOVE Mosaic place mat, page 106.

*LEFT Sea-washed
glass & shell
lamp, page 118.
ABOVE Mosaic
urn, page 114.
RIGHT More ideas
for decorated jars,
page 122.*

mosaic place mat

Broken and chipped plates can be given a second chance by turning them into a mosaic place mat or pan stand. Use one whole plate or an assortment of broken china in blue and white to create a pleasing arrangement. A broken family favourite from the past can become an heirloom of the future.

YOU WILL NEED

Goggles

Hammer

Patterned plate. (One with a picture is easier to use than one with a repeat pattern, as it is simple to jigsaw it back together again.)

Tile clippers

Circle of MDF 3cm (1¼in) wider than the plate to stick the mosaic to, or use an existing place mat.

Tile adhesive

Glass nuggets

Grout

Sponge

1 Wearing goggles, hammer the plate into large chunks. Reconstruct the plate and then hammer each large piece into smaller, fairly regular sized pieces.

3 Cover the MDF with tile adhesive to a thickness of 4mm (¼in). Starting with the border, place the broken pieces in position round the edge of the mat. Leave a small gap between each piece to allow for grouting. Then position the central picture. The adhesive is workable for up to 20 minutes, long enough for the mosaic to be adjusted.

2 Keeping the goggles on and using tile clippers, cut the curved area (the white bit in this case) away from the plate. You will be left with mainly the flat centre and rim of the plate.

4 Push glass nuggets into the tile adhesive in the gap left between the centre and the border of the mat. Spread the grout over the whole mat, making sure it is compressed into the crevices between the china fragments to give a smooth surface. Gently wipe off any excess using a damp sponge.

glass
light-pull

Add a touch of tactile luxury to any room with this splendid glass lightpull. Hang one in the bedroom, made from coloured glass beads that suit your design scheme, and your dreams. For more light-pull ideas, turn to page 110. They are so easy to make that soon you will have created a custom-made pull for every room in your house.

YOU WILL NEED

*Glass beads
(broken necklaces are ideal)*

*Chain the length you want
the finished light-pull to be,
minus the handle*

Fine wire

Pin-nosed pliers

1 Using the existing fittings on the beads, attach them to the chain. Open each fitting with pin-nosed pliers, then use them to close it round the chain.

2 I used a glass accumulator for the handle, but chunky beads wired together would work just as well. Attach handle to the chain with more wire.

3 If some beads don't have any fittings, wire them to the chain. Use a fine wire, such as florist's or craft wire to do this. Cut off any surplus wire with the pliers.

4 For an added detail, make a little symmetrical arrangement of beads on a loop of wire and attach it to the end of the light-pull.

More ideas for light-pulls

Let your imagination run wild and create your own lightpulls from almost anything around you.

LEFT TO RIGHT
• *Marbles stuck together with very strong glass glue and hung from wire and cord.*

• *Ribbon knotted between coins which have holes in their centres.*
• *An old compass hung from decorative cord.*

- A stone from the beach
  wrapped with wire and
  hung from a plug chain.
- Nuggets and marbles
  glued together and hung
  from ribbon.

- Bells tied to thick cord.
- Beads threaded onto fine
  cord and finished with
  a glass bauble.

- Antique pepperpot filled
  with pearl beads and hung
  from a ribbon.
- Beads and a glass bauble.
- An old key tied to a length
  of pretty ribbon.

china & glass

....

jam jar lantern

Make this lantern from an old jam jar. Mine is filled with sea-washed glass, but you could also use pebbles or gravel. Make a few and light a pathway on a summer's evening, or just make one or two and light up your bathroom while you take a candlelit dip.

YOU WILL NEED

Jam jar

75cm (29in) of wire

100cm (39in) of nautical rope

Scissors

Glue gun

Sea-washed glass

Nightlight candle

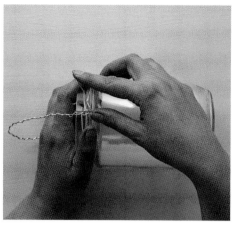

1 Tie the wire around the indent just below the rim of the jar. Take one of the loose ends over to the opposite side to form a handle and wind it around the tied piece to secure it. Then, wind the remaining piece of loose wire around the handle to strengthen it.

2 Tie the rope in a reef knot around the jar, with the knot itself at the front. Take the loose ends back around the jar and tie another reef knot at the back, as shown. Cut off any surplus rope.

3 Slide the rope down the jar a little way. Run a line of glue around the jar where you want the rope to sit, then slide the rope back up over the glue.

4 Put a layer of sea-washed glass in the bottom of the jar. Add a nightlight candle and then add a few more bits of the glass around the outside of the nightlight. Put a candle inside the jar and light it carefully. Remember never to leave a lighted candle in a draft or unattended.

mosaic urn

This pretty pink and white urn makes a proud statement, so use it to hold your finest blooms. Encrusted with colourful mosaic pieces and decorated with a broken brooch, you would never guess that its basis is a plain garden urn. For a variation on the theme, you could use glass nuggets, or broken china.

YOU WILL NEED

Urn

Clear glass beads

Waterproof silicone glue

Brooch

Mosaic pieces

Plastic spatula

Grout

Cloth

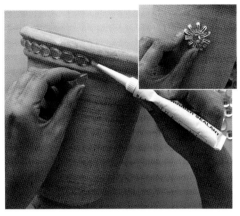

1 Start at the top of the urn and, using the silicone glue, attach a row of clear glass beads. Then, glue the brooch onto the centre of the urn (*see inset*).

3 Cover the whole urn with grout, applying it with the plastic spatula. Use the spatula to force the grout right down in between the pieces of mosaic.

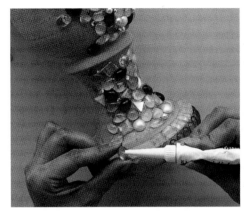

2 To pick out the rim of the base, use the same coloured pieces right around it. Glue the coloured mosaic pieces all over the main body of the urn, mixing up the colours randomly. Leave the glue to set.

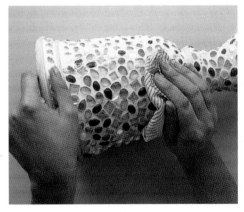

4 Wipe off any surplus grout with a damp cloth. When the grout is completely dry rub over the urn with a dry cloth to remove any remnants of grout on the mosaic pieces.

plate mirror

This rather gypsy-style mirror is simply made from an old blue and white plate and is decorated with a necklace and some green glass pieces I found in an antiques fair. However, you could use any plate with a patterned rim and glue on glass nuggets to decorate it further.

YOU WILL NEED

Plate

Mirror to fit centre of the plate

Strong glue (I used a glue gun)

Glass decorations or large glass nuggets

Necklace

Sticky plate hanger

1 Using the glue gun, apply lots of glue to the back of the mirror and glue it to the centre of the plate. Leave it to dry.

3 Glue the necklace to the edge of the mirror. Glue the centre of the necklace in place, then glue each end of the necklace round until the ends meet, leaving a gap large enough to take one bead. Remove any beads surplus to the length required. Tie the necklace ends into a secure knot. Trim the threads short and glue a bead over the knot. Remove any surplus glue.

2 Position the glass decorations around the edge of the plate at regular intervals and glue them in place. Leave them to dry.

4 To enable you to hang the mirror on the wall, attach a sticky plate hanger to the centre back of the plate, following the manufacturer's instructions.

sea-washed glass & shell lamp

At every beach I have ever visited I have managed to find some sea-washed glass. It appears in various colours, but mainly in lovely soft shades of green. A day spent on the seashore is not long enough to collect sufficient glass for this project, but a collection of sea-washed glass can be added to and collecting it, and pretty seashells, makes a walk on the beach even more interesting.

YOU WILL NEED

Lamp with plain cream-coloured shade

Paint, if the lamp base is not the colour of sea glass.

Glue gun

Seashells

Fine drill bit

Skewer

Fine wire

Wire cutters

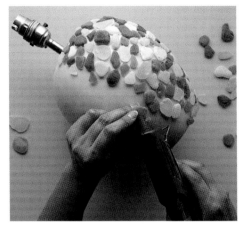

1 Paint the base if necessary and glue the pieces of glass to the lamp base. Just fit in bits as you go, leaving a small gap between each one.

2 Drill a hole into the top of each shell, where it is thickest. Be careful when doing this as the drill can slip.

3 Punch small holes around the bottom edge of the shade at regular intervals using the skewer.

4 Thread short lengths of fine wire through a shell, then through a hole in the lampshade and twist the ends together at the back. Cut off any surplus wire.

china & glass

gilded jar

It is surprisingly easy to gild a glass jar. Once you have done one you will want to do more. Here's a good one to start off with: a storage jar decorated with a simple, but lively, fish to keep in the bathroom. For more inspiration, turn to page 122.

YOU WILL NEED
Glass jar

Fish template, page 126

Masking tape

Fine paintbrush

Gold size

Gold leaf

Large paintbrush

Gold leaf sealer

1 Enlarge the template to the required size. Slip it inside the jar and stick it in place with some small pieces of masking tape.

3 Take a piece of gold leaf and lay it over the sized area. Rub the paper backing to ensure that the leaf is well stuck to the size. Peel off the backing.

2 Using the small paintbrush, outline the fish design in gold size onto the outside of the jar. Leave to dry until clear and tacky.

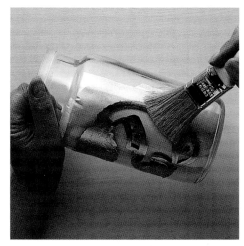

4 Brush off any excess leaf with the large paintbrush then seal the design with gold leaf sealer. The jar is now splash-proof, but it should not be immersed in water.

more ideas for decorated jars

Gild a series of jars to hold bathroom paraphernalia. You can decorate anything from precious cut-glass to humble jam jars to hold shampoo, bath oils, lotions and potions.

LEFT TO RIGHT
Large glass jar with gilded stripe and lid.
Frosted bottle with a metal tassel and sea washed glass *stuck on with waterproof silicone glue.*
Freehand gilded leaf

china & glass

● Striped vase decorated by
  masking off stripes and
  gilding in between them.
● Freehand gilded feather

TEMPLATES

buttoned pin-cushion, **page 16**

*hot-water bottle
cover,* **page 84**

stamp finger plate,
page 38

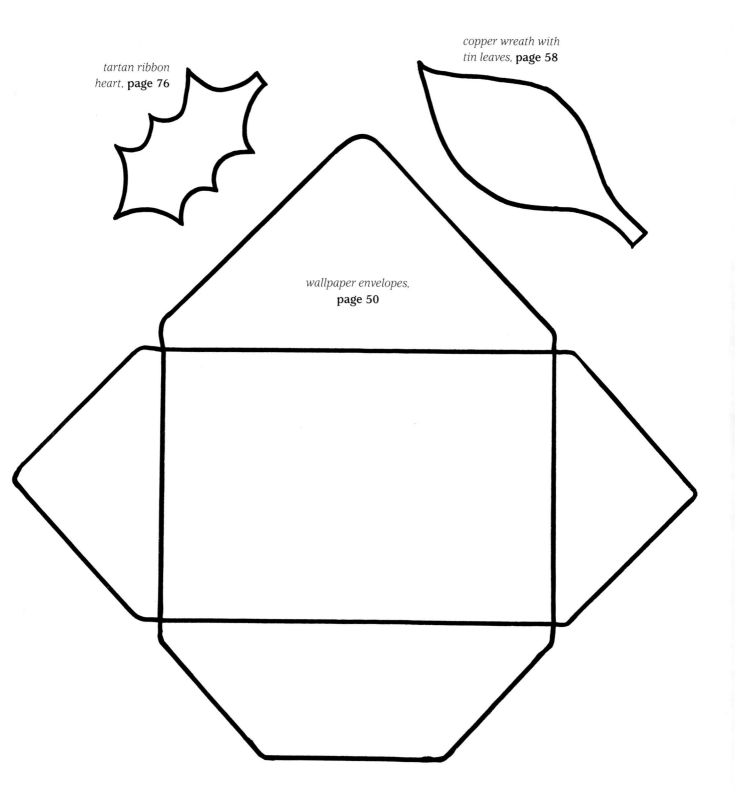

tartan ribbon heart, **page 76**

copper wreath with tin leaves, **page 58**

wallpaper envelopes, **page 50**

wire plant support, **page 64**

gilded jar, **page 120**

pumpkin crate, **page 100**

templates

suppliers

Flea markets, antiques fairs, carboot sales and junk shops should be your first port of call when collecting materials for any of these projects, otherwise try the following suppliers.

Homecraft Direct
PO Box 38
Leicester
LE1 9BU
0116-251 3139
Craft materials by mail order

A Wild Bunch
220 Merton High Street
London
SW19 1AU
020-8288 9058
Preserved plant materials
Mail order available

Ells and Farrier
01494-715606
Beads and trimmings
Mail order available

Garden Care Supplies Ltd
Old Kingston Road
Worcester Park
Surrey
KT4 7QH
0202-8337 9922
Garden supplies

The Packhouse Antiques Centre
Tongham Road
Farnham
Surrey
GU10 1PQ
01252-781 010
86 stalls selling quality antiques

VV Rouleaux
54 Sloane Square
Cliveden Place
London
SW1W 8AX
020-7730 3125
Ribbons, braids and trimmings

Wickes Building Supplies UK
Call 020-8901 2000 for branches
General DIY materials

author's acknowledgements

Firstly I would like to thank my good friend Kate Haxell, who has been involved with this book from its very beginning and has made the whole process of a first book less daunting by her support, good humour and vast knowledge of the process. I would also like to thank Kate Kirby who has been an absolute joy to work with and to whom I'm very grateful. Also, many thanks to Ruth Hope, who has kindly put together clear, lovely layouts. A huge thank you to my partner, Ling Wong, for all his creative input and for taking wonderful photographs of all my projects.

Thanks to my parents, Sally and Ray, and my brother, Paul, for all their continued support, and to my sister, Sam, a fellow collector and someone who never ceases to inspire me. Thank you to my grandmother, Freda, who has not only always encouraged me to make the most of any creativity I have, but who has trekked around various antique shops scouting out curious items for me to use.

I would also like to thank The Packhouse Antiques Centre for providing a photographic location for the *where to collect* pages and Garden Care Supplies for providing a photographic location for the *bamboo planter*. Joss and Josephine for their beautiful artwork used in the *buttoned cuffs & cushion* photograph.

index